WITHDRAWN

Damaged, Obsolete, or Surplus
Jackson County Library Services

D0579363

Transporte público
Public Transportation

¡VAMOS A TOMAR
EL AUTOBÚS!

LET'S RIDE THE
CITY BUS!

Elisa Peters

Traducido por Eida de la Veaa

JACKSON COUNTY LIBRARY, MEDFORD, OR

AUG   2014

press.

New York

Published in 2015 by The Rosen Publishing Group, Inc.
29 East 21st Street, New York, NY 10010

Copyright © 2015 by The Rosen Publishing Group, Inc.

All rights reserved. No part of this book may be reproduced in any form without permission in writing from the publisher, except by a reviewer.

First Edition

Editor: Amelie von Zumbusch
Photo Research: Katie Stryker
Book Design: Andrew Povolny

Spanish translation: Eida de la Vega

Photo Credits: Cover Richard Cummins/Lonely Planet Images/Getty Images; p. 5 Federico Rostagno/Shutterstock.com; p. 6 Photofusion/Contributor/Universal Images Group/Getty Images; p. 9 Matthew Gonzalez/E+/Getty Images; p. 10 iStock/Thinkstock; p. 13 Carmakoma/Shutterstock.com; p. 14 Science & Society Picture Library/Contributor/SSPL/Getty Images; p. 17 Miker/Shutterstock.com; p. 18 Chris Jenner/Shutterstock.com; p. 21 Tadeusz Lbrom/Shutterstock.com; p. 22 Stanislav Tiplyashin/Shutterstock.com.

Library of Congress Cataloging-in-Publication Data

Peters, Elisa, author.
 Let's ride the city bus! = ¡Vamos a tomar el autobús! / by Elisa Peters ; translated by Eida de la Vega – First edition.
    pages cm. – (Public transportation = Transporte público)
 English and Spanish.
 Includes index.
 ISBN 978-1-4777-6777-1 (library binding)
 1. Buses–Juvenile literature. I. Vega, Eida de la, translator. II. Peters, Elisa. Let's ride the city bus! III. Peters, Elisa. Let's ride the city bus! Spanish. IV. Title. V. Title: ¡Vamos a tomar el autobús!
 TL232.P44 2015
 629.28'333–dc23
                              2013046498

Websites: Due to the changing nature of Internet links, PowerKids Press has developed an online list of websites related to the subject of this book. This site is updated regularly. Please use this link to access the list: www.powerkidslinks.com/putr/cbus/

Manufactured in the United States of America

CPSIA Compliance Information: Batch #WS14PK4: For Further Information contact Rosen Publishing, New York, New York at 1-800-237-9932

Contenido

Contents

¿Alguna vez has tomado un autobús de la ciudad? También se les llama ómnibus.

Have you ever taken a city bus? "Bus" is short for "omnibus."

YOU CAN
NEW WOM

6

Espera por el autobús en la parada. Cuando el autobús llega, sube.

Wait at the bus stop. When the bus comes, get on.

¡Asegúrate de subir al autobús correcto! Un **letrero** en el frente indica el trayecto.

Make sure to get on the right bus! A **panel** on the front lists the route.

Pagas por viajar en el autobús. También puedes pagar con una **tarjeta de abono**.

You pay a fare to ride. You can often pay with a **transit pass**.

Presiona el botón o la cinta para dejarle saber al conductor que quieres bajarte en la próxima parada.

Press the button or tape to tell the driver you want to get off at the next stop.

14

Los caballos tiraban
de los primeros autobuses.
En la década de 1830,
llegaron los autobuses
impulsados por vapor.

Horses drew the first buses.
Next came steam-powered
buses in the 1830s.

Hoy en día, la mayoría de los autobuses utiliza gasolina. También hay autobuses híbridos que contaminan menos.

Today most buses run on gas. Hybrid buses are used, too. They pollute less.

18

Los autobuses de dos niveles se llaman autobuses de dos pisos.

Buses with two levels are double-decker buses.

Los **autobuses articulados** son muy largos. Sus dos partes se unen con una juntura móvil. Esto les da flexibilidad.

Articulated buses are extra long. Their two parts meet at a joint. This lets them bend.

¡Viajar en autobús es divertido!
Es una manera fácil
de moverte en tu ciudad
o pueblo.

Riding the bus is fun! It is an
easy way to get around your
city or town.

PALABRAS QUE DEBES SABER / WORDS TO KNOW

(el) autobús articulado

articulated bus

(el) letrero

panel

(la) tarjeta de abono

transit pass

ÍNDICE

INDEX